Contents

What is Buddhism?   4

Who was the Buddha?   6

Living the Buddhist path   8

Buddhism around the world   10

Places of worship   12

Family celebrations and rituals   14

Festivals and traditions   16

The Mani Man   18

Important people   20

Sacred texts   22

Holy places   24

Art and craft   26

Activities   28

Glossary   30

Index   31

Notes for parents and teachers   32

What is Buddhism?

Buddhism is a way of life that follows the teachings of the Buddha (see pages 6–7). Buddhists believe that everyone has a **Buddha nature** that is kind and wise, and clear like pure water. Unhelpful emotions such as anger, hatred and greed make the mind cloudy like muddy water. The more cloudy our minds become, the more problems we encounter. Buddhists believe that it is possible to become happier and calmer by clearing our minds of unhelpful thoughts through **meditation**.

Training the mind

The Buddha discovered how to clear his mind. People saw how kind, wise, happy and peaceful he had become and asked the Buddha to teach them how to clear their minds, too. The Buddha taught many different methods to help people. He advised people to meditate and to examine his methods to see if they worked. He told them to question his ideas, too.

◀ Statues of the Buddha remind his followers that they can learn to be peaceful.

Buddhism

Kevin and Denise Fossey

QED Publishing

Copyright © QED Publishing 2006

First published in the UK in 2006 by
QED Publishing
A Quarto Group company
226 City Road
London EC1V 2TT
www.qed-publishing.co.uk

Reprinted in 2007

A catalogue record for this book is available from the British Library.

ISBN 978 1 84538 711 2

Written by Kevin and Denise Fossey
Designed by Tall Tree Books
Editor Louisa Somerville
Consultant John Keast
Illustrations Laure Fournier

Publisher Steve Evans
Creative Director Zeta Davies
Editorial Director Jean Coppendale

Printed and bound in China

Picture credits
Key: t = top, b = bottom, c = centre, l = left, r = right, FC = front cover

Alamy/Don Jon Red 15t/ Maciej Wotjkowiak 12; **Ark Religion**/Andrea Alborno 20
/ Tibor Bognar 8, 9, 10, 11t, 22/ Roger Cracknell 13b/ Dinodia Photo Library 5t, 7b,
24bl, br/ Fiona Good 16, 25b/ Jeff Greenberg 13t/ Douglas Houghton 27/ Francoise
Pirson 1/ Helene Rogers 6, 7t, 14/ Jane Sweeney 4; **Corbis**/Brecelj Bojan 27tr/ Richard
Krause/Reuters 26/Colin McPherson 21tr/ ML Sinibaldi 15b/ Ahmad Yusni/epa 17;
Getty Images/D.E.Cox 11b/ Gavin Hellier FC/ Bill Wassmann 25t.

Words in **bold** are explained
in the glossary on page 30.

The Wheel of Teaching

The symbol of Buddhism is the Dharma Wheel, or Buddhist Wheel of Teaching. It is the symbol of the Eightfold Path, the Buddhist cure for suffering (see page 8). The Three Jewels spiral is in the centre of the wheel. All Buddhists believe the Three Jewels are important. The Three Jewels are the Buddha (who gave teachings), the **Dharma** (the teachings of the Buddha) and the Sangha (the followers of Buddhism). Although the Buddha was human, he found that he could overcome anger and greed. The Dharma tells us how to do this and the Sangha keep us company on the path.

▲ The eight spokes on the Dharma Wheel represent the Eightfold Path.

The Three Poisons

The Buddha explained that the difficulties of life go on and on. He said that we could train our minds to develop helpful qualities, such as patience, **compassion** and forgiveness. Then eventually we will be free of suffering. He said:

"The Three Poisons that make us unhappy are greed, anger and ignorance."

Meditation experiment

You will need: clean glass jar • soil • water • dessert spoon

1 Put a spoonful of soil into a jar. Add water and stir. The water will become cloudy.

2 Check your water mixture. Does the water become clear again?

3 Eventually, the soil settles and the water becomes clearer. In meditation, our emotions settle and our minds become clearer. To remove all the soil, we need a filter. To remove unhelpful thoughts, Buddhists use the Eightfold path.

Who was the Buddha?

The Buddha was born a prince 2500 years ago in Lumbini, Nepal. It is said that at the moment of his birth, peace and happiness spread throughout the land. At that time, his name was Prince Siddhartha Gautama. The king wanted his son to become a great ruler, so he surrounded Siddhartha with luxury, flowers and music. He was not allowed to see any suffering at all.

▼ A holy man gazed at the baby and said, "If the Prince leaves the Kingdom and learns of life's sorrows, he will become a wise man and teach people to live in peace."

The Four Sights

When he grew up, Siddhartha wondered what life outside the palace was like. He pleaded with his father to let him explore. In the city, he saw a sick person, an old person and a dead person. He had never seen suffering before and was shocked. Siddhartha saw that all life on Earth struggled to survive. He wished he could help everyone. Then, finally, he saw a holy man who had given up everything to try to find perfect happiness. 'This is what I can do,' thought Siddhartha. 'I will give up my luxuries and search for true happiness and the end of suffering for all beings.'

The Middle Way

As he travelled, Siddhartha met several **ascetics** (holy men) who believed that if they could master pain, their suffering would end. Siddhartha tried their methods. For months, he went without food, sleep or shelter. This bought him no success and he was close to death. One day, a young woman gave him a bowl of milk. When he had drunk it all, he felt strong again. He realized then that he had found the path out of suffering. He would call it the Middle Way – a life of moderation, without luxury, but also without unnecessary hardship.

▲ The young woman, called Sujata, thought Siddhartha was a tree spirit. She offered him a bowl of rice milk.

◄ Buddha sits under a Bodhi tree and becomes enlightened.

Enlightenment

Siddhartha went to the town of Bodh Gaya in India and sat under a **Bodhi tree** to meditate, to find a way out of suffering. After 49 days and nights he became **enlightened** – he had found the answer to his quest. Siddhartha then became the Buddha, the 'enlightened one'. He realized that he was now like a doctor who knew which medicine people needed to cure them of their suffering. When the Buddha died, at the age of 80, he had reached a state called Nirvana, which is a state of perfect bliss and happiness.

7

Living the Buddhist path

For 40 years after his enlightenment, the Buddha taught people how to be free from their suffering. He gave his first teachings at Sarnath, an ancient holy site. He drew a wheel and explained the cycle of birth, life, death and rebirth. These teachings were called the Four Noble Truths.

The Four Noble Truths

1. Life contains disappointment and suffering.
2. The causes of suffering are greed, and dissatisfaction with what we have.
3. It is possible to become cured.
4. If we follow the Middle Way, we will find a cure for suffering.

The Eightfold Path (or Middle Way)

The Buddha taught an eightfold path, a 'middle way' between luxury and hardship.

1. Right Understanding. To hear, see and understand the Four Noble Truths.
2. Right Thought. To be unselfish and develop compassion.
3. Right Speech. To be truthful, using our words carefully and wisely and not gossiping about others.
4. Right Action. To be kind and thoughtful, using the Five Precepts as a guide.
5. Right Livelihood. To do work that helps people, animals or the planet. To avoid jobs that cause harm or damage.
6. Right Effort. To be aware of ourselves and our fe... to change sad, fear... moods into happy, calm ones.
7. Right Mindfulness. ... present moment ... interest in everyth...
8. Right Concentrati... meditation to dev... and positive min...

The Five Precepts – a guide for living

Many Buddhists try to keep to the Buddha's 'Five Precepts', which give a guide for living. The precepts are:

1. Take care of all living things. Don't harm people, animals or plants and care for them as we would be cared for ourselves.

2. Respect property and the environment. Don't take things that belong to others, and ask when borrowing and sharing.

3. Be responsible for ourselves and our relationships. Care for our friends and respect others, even if they are not our friends.

4. Keep the body healthy and the mind clear. Don't cloud the mind with drugs or alcohol.

5. Speak kindly and honestly. Be careful with the use of speech and voice.

▲ On festival days, Buddhists may visit a temple and promise to follow the Five Precepts.

◄ Monks working in a temple. Whatever work monks do, they are taught to do it with their full attention.

9

Buddhism around the world

Scholars, **philosophers** and holy men from many countries came to India to listen to the Buddha's wisdom. Then they travelled far and wide to share his teachings. It is said that the Buddha gave 84 000 teachings to help different people. This resulted in Buddhism being practised in a variety of ways in different countries. All Buddhists, however, celebrate the Three Jewels, which give them inspiration, strength and guidance (see page 5). They follow the Five Precepts (see page 9) and try to help all human beings, animals and the environment.

Theravada Buddhism

This type of Buddhism is followed in Sri Lanka, Thailand, Laos, Burma and Cambodia. Theravada Buddhism is close to the lifestyle of the Buddha. Theravada **monks** and **nuns** educate people and offer valuable advice. They do not use or handle money, so the local community supports them, by providing them with food and other essentials for living. If no one gives them food, they do not eat.

◀ The little boy is helping his mother give food to the Buddhist nuns.

Zen Buddhism

Zen developed in Japan. Zen means 'contemplation'. This form of Buddhism is based on strict mental training in order to help meditation, to become enlightened. Zen is based on simplicity. Zen Buddhists read texts and use martial arts, paintings, poems and hard or impossible questions called **koans** to help concentrate their minds.

◀ The gravel in this Zen garden has been carefully raked to look like water.

Buddhism in the West

Buddhism has spread widely beyond Asia and there are now many Theravada, Mahayana and Zen Buddhist centres in the West. The Friends of the Western Buddhist Order, which was created for Western culture, places great importance on 'right livelihood' (see page 8). Members organize community shops selling fair-trade goods and support educational and charitable projects worldwide.

▲ A novice monk at his school desk in the Drepung Monastery in Lhasa, Tibet.

Mahayana Buddhism

Found in Tibet, India, Nepal, Mongolia and China, Mahayana Buddhists believe in developing qualities of wisdom, patience, kindness and compassion both in themselves and others. Their goal is to be a **Bodhisattva**, one who dedicates their life and future lives to the welfare of others.

11

Places of worship

Buddhist **temples** vary in style and appearance. Tibetan temples (or gompas) are ornate with highly decorated **thangkas**, (holy pictures, see page 26), statues and shrines. In the Zen tradition, the temples tend to be simple and spacious. In the Western Buddhist tradition people usually visit a simple shrine in a Buddhist centre.

Peace and tranquillity

Before entering the main hall of a temple people remove their shoes. When they see the Buddha statue many Buddhists bow to give thanks for the teachings and pay their respects. They may make offerings or just sit quietly. An atmosphere of peace and tranquillity is present in a Buddhist temple or **monastery**.

▼ Kuchary Buddhist Centre, Poland. Many Buddhists like to meditate in the open air just as the Buddha did.

The shrine

On a shrine in a temple, as well as the Buddha statue, there will usually be a candle or lamp. This represents the Buddha's wisdom and the lighting up of our minds. There are also flowers to remind people of the Buddha's teaching on **impermanence** and change because they grow and then fade away. The sweet smell of **incense** spreads to all parts of the building. In the same way, good actions and deeds spread to others, having a positive influence on both the local community and the world.

▲ A man kneels before an elaborately decorated shrine in Chinatown, New York City.

Prayer wheels

In Tibetan Buddhist temples you will see prayer wheels. They contain prayers for the happiness of all people, written millions of times. People spin the wheels to add power to the prayers. Some wheels are huge and reach from floor to ceiling. Others can be held in the hand.

▲ When the prayer wheel is turned, the power of the prayers increases to help all beings.

Offerings

People who visit a shrine may give candles, flowers or incense in thanks for the Buddha's teachings, which help them in their lives. When visiting a monastery they may give money and food, to support the monks and nuns.

13

Family celebrations and rituals

The Buddha taught that everything changes all the time. He encouraged people to investigate his teachings and to adapt them to suit their needs. Celebrations vary in different Buddhist traditions and communities. In the West, monks, nuns and lay people (those who are not monks and nuns) have created ceremonies to suit a Western lifestyle.

Birth

In Theravadan communities (see page 10) a naming ceremony is held at home when a baby is born. The monk or nun leading the ceremony reminds the guests of the Buddha's teachings – that all people are connected and all must be a good friend to the child. Buddhists do this by developing kindness, patience, compassion and courage. A cotton thread is wound around the baby's wrist as a blessing, where it stays until it falls off naturally.

▼ A priest blesses a baby during a naming ceremony.

14

Lighting candles

Most Buddhists have a shrine at home with a Buddha statue, and perhaps a picture of their Buddhist teacher and some flowers. Many Buddhists light a candle before they pray or meditate.

▲ A girl makes an offering at a shrine in her home.

Death

The Buddha taught that people are fortunate to have human lives. They are free to train themselves, develop and improve. Buddhists are encouraged to use their time well because we do not know when we will die. Many Buddhists believe in **reincarnation**, or rebirth. When someone dies, monks, nuns or lay people give prayers for a good rebirth.

◀ A Buddhist wedding on the island of Sri Lanka.

Marriage

Buddhists may get married at home or at a temple. Each country has very different customs for the ceremony. Most Buddhists like to have a blessing from a monk or a nun for their wedding. Prayers are often chanted and there is usually a party afterwards.

Festivals and traditions

The various groups of Buddhists in different countries celebrate festivals in their own ways. Many festivals celebrate the Buddha's life, teaching and enlightenment (see page 7).

▼ Masked dancers performing at the festival of Losar.

Losar

Tibetan Buddhists celebrate New Year in February at a festival called Losar, which lasts for several days. Before Losar everything is cleaned and buildings are painted. During Losar monks and nuns wear their best robes and **prayer flags** are tied to the monasteries and put up on mountains. Prayers are said and hundreds of **butter lamps** are lit. Monks dressed in huge masks and colourful costumes perform Buddhist dances, plays or operas for the public.

Wesak

Theravada Buddhists celebrate Wesak on the day of the full moon in May. It reminds Buddhists of the Buddha's birth, enlightenment and death. Light – symbolizing enlightenment and the Buddha's teaching bringing light to the world – forms an important part of Wesak. Candles are lit, Buddha statues are surrounded with lights and there are processions with lanterns. Senior monks and nuns give teachings and, as it gets dark, a candlelit meditation is held.

▲ Wesak celebration at the Dharma School, U.K. Everyone writes a prayer on a paper Bodhi leaf and helps to paint a Peace Mandala.

Hana Matsuri

The Japanese flower festival of Hana Matsuri celebrates the Buddha's birth and the coming of spring. A model of the infant Buddha is placed in a floral shrine to create a scene of his birth at the beautiful gardens of Lumbini (see page 24). The festival is held on the 8 April each year.

Kathina

The festival of Kathina celebrates the Sangha, the entire community of Buddhists – monks, nuns and lay people. In countries such as Thailand, Cambodia, Laos and Sri Lanka, Kathina marks the end of the rainy season when heavy monsoon rains make it difficult for monks and nuns to travel to teach. Kathina is celebrated in October and lay people offer gifts of robes, food or items for the monastery, to help the monks and nuns to live through the following year.

The Mani Man

The Mani Man lived with his son on a small farm. He was called the Mani Man because he could often be seen and heard reciting his prayers and counting them on his special mala beads. "Om Mani Padme Hung" was his special prayer, hence his nickname 'The Mani Man'. His wife had died and his son was kept busy looking after the small farm and their one horse.

One day, the boy awoke to find that their fine horse had disappeared overnight. The father and son looked everywhere but the horse was nowhere to be seen. Neighbours came to say how sorry they were that the animal had gone but the old man just kept on repeating his prayers. When people tried to sympathize with his loss, he said, "Who knows what is good or bad? We shall see what we shall see, Om Mani Padme Hung."

A few days later the horse returned, with two other horses it had met in the hills. The son was happy to have his horse back and the neighbours came and said how lucky the man and son were to have two more strong horses. The old man carried on saying his prayers. When people got excited, he just said, "Who knows what is good or bad? We shall see what we shall see, Om Mani Padme Hung."

One of the new horses was very wild and, while the son was trying to tame the creature, it reared up and the boy fell and broke his leg. Neighbours came to say how shocked they were to hear about this dreadful accident. The old man just kept saying his prayers. When the neighbours were sad, he said, "Who knows what is good or bad? We shall see what we shall see, Om Mani Padme Hung."

Soon some soldiers came looking for young men to fight in the army. They took all the young men, but the son with the broken leg was left at home. The neighbours came and said how lucky he was to have a broken leg. The old man just kept saying his prayers and said, "Who knows what is good or bad? We shall see what we shall see, Om Mani Padme Hung."

The story tells us that in life there is both happiness and suffering. We all experience them, but what seems bad may turn out to be good.

'Om Mani Padme Hung' is the national prayer of Tibet. Many Tibetans say the prayer hundreds of times a day to try and free others from suffering.

Important people

Each strand of Buddhism has its own leaders and teachers. They inspire their followers, teach **non-violence** and take the path of kindness and peace.

The Venerable Ani Tenzin Palmo

Born in London, Britain, Ani Tenzin Palmo became a nun in the Tibetan Buddhist tradition at the age of 21. With her teacher's guidance, she lived and meditated alone for 12 years in a cave 4000m up in the Himalayan mountains, India. Since then, she has set up schools and Buddhist centres.

The Dalai Lama

The leader of Tibetan Buddhism, Tibet and the Tibetan people is the Dalai Lama. Dalai Lama means 'ocean of wisdom'. Thousands of people come to hear him teach although he is very humble, describing himself as a simple Buddhist monk. He lives in **exile** in India, as he fled Tibet when it was invaded by the Chinese in 1959. A child once asked him how he could live his life in the best possible way. The Dalai Lama replied, "If you can help others this is very good. If you cannot do this, at least do not harm them."

▼ His Holiness the Dalai Lama says, "My religion is simple, my religion is kindness."

Thich Nhat Hanh

A Vietnamese Zen master, poet and man of peace, Thich Nhat Hanh travels the world teaching peace and forgiveness, and has helped many **refugees** and homeless people. He teaches about living in the present moment. "Peace is all around us, in the world and in nature and within us, in our bodies and our spirits," he says.

▲ Buddhists studying religious teachings while on retreat at Holy Island, Scotland.

The Venerable Ajahn Chah

Ajahn Chah was a Thai Theravada meditation master. He lived a simple life in the forests of North-east Thailand. He inspired many Buddhists around the world and helped to set up a Theravada community in Britain. Buddhists believe that nothing is fixed or permanent. Ajahn Chah said, "Take trees… first they come into being, then they grow and mature, always changing until they finally die as every tree must. In the same way, people and animals are born, grow and change during their lifetimes until they eventually die. This shows the Way of Dharma. All things are impermanent."

Retreats

Many Buddhists take the time to meditate, reflect, pray and study away from the routine of their usual lives. This is called a retreat. Retreats can last for just a day, for a week, for a year, for three years or even for twelve years. A retreat may be solitary or with a group of people. Some retreats are silent while others involve discussion.

21

Sacred texts

To begin with, the teachings of Buddha were passed down by word of mouth. Four hundred years after his death, the Theravadan Sangha in Sri Lanka, decided to write the teachings down. The texts were written in the Pali language of Sri Lanka and are called the Pali Canon.

The Three Baskets

The Pali teachings were written on palm leaves and stored in baskets, so they became known as The Three Baskets. In the first basket were kept the rules for the monks and nuns, the second basket held the teachings of the Buddha and the third basket contained explanations of the teachings.

▼ Tibetan prayer flags traditionally hang from monastery rooftops or from posts placed high up in the Himalayan mountains.

Prayers

Prayers are an important part of Buddhist practice. They help to focus the mind and calm us if we become upset, worried, frightened or over-excited. Tibetan prayer flags often have a drawing, called a Wind Horse, on them. It symbolizes **uplifting energy** that carries good fortune to everyone. Western Buddhists often use prayer flags at fairs and charity events.

A popular Buddhist prayer:

"May all beings have happiness and the cause of happiness, may they be free from suffering and the cause of suffering."

Make a Tibetan prayer flag

You will need: 5 rectangular sheets of yellow, green, red, white and blue paper • pencil • felt-tip pens • sticky tape • string

The different colours represent natural elements: yellow (earth), green (water), red (fire), white (cloud) and blue (sky).

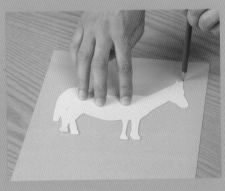

May all people be happy, live in peace and have enough to eat.

1 Draw a horse on the top half of each flag. What do your Wind Horses look like? You could use a stencil or you can make each horse look different.

2 Write a prayer on each flag. Make up different ones, such as 'May all people be happy.' or 'I wish everyone had enough to eat.' Decorate your flags with patterns and symbols.

3 Put the flags, face down, in this order: yellow, green, red, white, blue. Run the string just under the top edge of each flag. Fold each flag over the string and tape down. Hang the flags.

Holy places

There are holy places that are special to Buddhists. The Buddha encouraged his followers to visit these places as a **pilgrimage**, to show their commitment to their faith. When Buddhists make a pilgrimage, they feel inspired to practise what the Buddha taught.

The Buddha's birthplace

The Buddha was born under a tree in a beautiful garden in Lumbini, in Nepal around 563 BCE. Today, many Buddhist **pilgrims** visit the remains of the sacred garden and see the pool where, it is said, Buddha's mother bathed before she gave birth. Several shrines have been built here by Buddhists and their supporters.

▲ Lumbini Garden, the Buddha's birthplace in Nepal.

► Buddhist monks and pilgrims visit Lumbini Garden for inspiration and quiet contemplation.

Mount Kailas

The magnificent Mount Kailas, in Tibet, is sacred to both Hindus and Buddhists. Pilgrims walk the kora (circular path) around the mountain. This path is 55km long and climbs up to 6000m at its highest point. It is said that if you walk the path 108 times, then you will reach Nirvana and become completely at peace with the Universe.

▲ Mount Kailas is also important to followers of other religions, such as Hinduism and Jainism.

◄ Buddhist monks at prayer in front of the Mahabodhi Temple in Bodh Gaya.

Bodh Gaya

Thousands of Buddhist pilgrims from around the world visit Bodh Gaya, in India. This is where the Buddha became enlightened while sitting under a tree. Pilgrims come here to see an ancient Bodhi tree which is said to have grown from the tree the Buddha sat under. They also follow the path around a historic Mahabodhi Temple, reciting prayers. Meditation centres have been built nearby where visitors can learn from great Buddhist teachers.

Sacred water

Four of the great rivers that flow through Asia start near Mount Kailas. Millions of people can eat, drink and survive because of the water in these mighty rivers. Zen poet Thich Nhat Hanh (see page 21) writes:

"Water flows from high in the mountains. Water runs deep in the Earth. Miraculously, water comes to us, And sustains all life."

25

Art and craft

The oldest types of Buddhist art were painted on cave walls or carved in stone. They showed events from the Buddha's life. These scenes were sometimes shown as a series of **symbols** such as a footprint, a wheel, a Bodhi tree, a lotus flower or a **stupa**.

The Zen arts

Zen (see page 11) expresses simplicity in art. Painting, calligraphy (beautiful writing), poetry, music and gardening are aspects of Zen art. The artist attempts to express the Buddha nature in ordinary things.

Thangka paintings

Thangkas are a Tibetan tradition. Each one will show a picture of the Buddha and a scene from his life or an event from the life of another important Buddhist teacher. Thangkas often have complex designs and are painted onto fine cotton or silk. Thangkas can be huge, sometimes large enough to cover the outside of a monastery.

▲ This huge Thangka is displayed each year during Monlam, the great prayer festival.

Sand mandalas

Sand **mandalas** are symbolic patterns made with brightly coloured sand. Sometimes they are made at Buddhist exhibitions or Tibetan cultural events. Crowds of visitors watch the monks pile the sand into elaborate designs. After a few days, the sand is swept away to remind us that everything changes and nothing lasts forever.

▲ Monks use metal funnels to position the coloured sand. They begin the design in the middle and work outwards.

Statues

Buddha statues come in many styles and the positions of their hands have different meanings. Many Buddhist statues are of Bodhisattvas and great teachers. They can be made of wood, stone or metal and sometimes contain important prayers.

▶ The hand of this statue of the Buddha from Hong Kong, China, is in the position for teaching.

Wall hangings

Tibetan refugee communities make wall hangings decorated with Buddhist designs or inspiring words, such as these by the Dalai Lama:

"Never give up,
No matter what is going on.
Never give up.
Be compassionate,
Not just to your friends
But to everyone.
Be compassionate.
Work for peace,
In your heart and in the world.
Work for peace,
And I say again
Never give up.
No matter what is happening,
No matter what is going on around you,
Never give up."

27

Activities

Make a Buddha mobile

You will need: thin card • paints or crayons • glitter • glue • felt-tip pens • scissors • coloured thread or string

What qualities do you think the Buddha has? Write down some words that describe the Buddha.

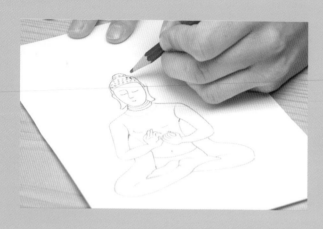

1 Draw a picture of the Buddha onto white card.

2 Cut out the Buddha, leaving a border all around. Colour in your Buddha using coloured pencils. When finished, turn the card over and draw the same Buddha on the back. Colour in.

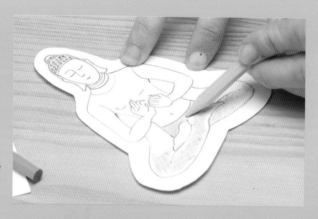

3 Draw four ovals onto white card. Copy the words shown in the picture onto each one with a black felt-tip pen. Cut the ovals out.

peace

patience

help others

happiness

4 Use felt-tip pens to colour the edges of each oval. With a sharp pencil, make a small hole at the bottom of the Buddha, the top and bottom of three ovals and the top of the fourth oval. Thread string through the holes and knot the ends.

Make Tibetan offering rice

You will need: 225g long grain rice • saucepan • sieve • bowl • 100g butter • wooden spoon • 50g raisins • 100g soft light brown sugar • saucers

This dish is often served to honoured guests. This recipe makes 18 small portions.

1 Following the instructions on the packet, boil or steam the rice until it's cooked. Drain the rice and put it in a bowl.

2 Melt the butter in a saucepan. Add the cooked rice to the melted butter and stir them together with a wooden spoon over a low heat.

3 Now mix in the raisins and sugar. Leave the mixture to cool.

4 Once it's cold, serve the rice mixture in a small bowl. Shape each portion into a mound, to look like a mountain.

Monks' food

In Buddhist communities, lay Buddhists donate food to the monks and nuns. Each monk or nun carries a bowl and walks slowly through the town. As they pass by, lay Buddhists put food in the bowls. This is called an **alms round**. The Buddha and his followers did the same 2500 years ago. The monks and nuns eat whatever they are given. Both savoury and sweet items go into the same bowl, so rice and curry may go in with strawberry cheesecake!

29

Glossary

alms round Monks and nuns walk around the local area with their empty bowls. Lay people put food in the bowls.

ascetic A person who does not allow any comforts in their search for truth.

Bodhi tree The tree under which the Buddha sat to attain bodhi (enlightenment).

Bodhisattva A person who wants to be enlightened so that he or she can help others.

Buddha nature Something pure, perfect and indestructable that is in everything.

butter lamp A small metal bowl filled with melted butter and a wick, lit like a candle.

compassion The wish to free others from suffering.

Dharma The teachings given by the Buddha.

enlightened To achieve the state of perfect understanding.

exile To live in another country because you cannot live in your own country.

impermanence The fact that nothing lasts forever, everything is always changing.

incense A dried plant mixture that releases a pleasant smell when lit.

koan A problem that has no obvious logical answer, such as: what is the sound of a single hand clapping?

mandala A design that symbolizes the universe. It gives off positive energy to the environment and to those who view it.

meditation To train the mind to become calm and clear.

monastery The building where monks and nuns live and study.

monks Male members of the Buddhist community who have taken vows. Monks usually wear robes.

non-violence Not using violence to solve disagreements with others.

nuns The female equivalent of monks.

philosopher Someone who studies and tries to answer questions about life.

pilgrimage A journey to a sacred place.

pilgrims People who go on a journey to visit a sacred place and show their devotion to their faith.

prayer flags Flags with symbols and prayers on them. They are said to bring happiness, long life and prosperity to all those nearby.

refugees People who have escaped from their own country due to danger.

reincarnation On the death of a body, the soul being born again in another body.

stupa A Buddhist monument, often dome-shaped, that usually contains prayers and relics of Buddhist teachers.

symbol An object or image that is used to suggest something else.

temple A building for prayer and ceremonies.

Thangkas Painted or emboidered artworks that are hung in a monastery or a family altar.

uplifting energy Helpful, positive energy that makes us feel alive.

Index

Ajhan Chah 21
alms round 29, 30
Ani Tenzin Palmo 20, 21
art 26-27
ascetic 7, 30

birth 14
Bodh Gaya 7, 25
Bodhisattva 11, 30
Bodhi tree 7, 30
Buddha 4, 6–7, 8, 10, 14, 15, 24
Buddha mind 4
Buddha mobile 28
Buddha nature 4, 26, 30
butter lamps 16, 30

celebrations 14–15
compassion 5, 30

Dalai Lama 20, 27
Dharma 5, 30

Eightfold Path 8
enlightened 7, 11, 30
exile 20, 30

festivals 16–17
Five Precepts 9
Four Noble Truths 9

Hana Matsuri 17

impermanence 13, 10
incense 13, 30
India 25

Japan 11, 17

Kathina 17
koans 11, 30

Losar 16
Lumbini 6, 17, 24

Mahayana Buddhism 11
mandalas 27, 30
Mani Man 18–19
marriage 15
martial arts 11
meditation 4, 5, 20, 21, 25, 30
monastery 12, 30
monks 8, 10, 14, 30
Mount Kailas 25

naming ceremony 14
Nepal 6, 11, 24
Nirvana 7, 25
non-violence 20, 30
nuns 10, 14, 30

offerings 13, 29

philosopher 10, 30
pilgrimage 24, 30
pilgrims 24, 25, 30
prayer 15, 22, 23
prayer flags 16, 22, 23, 30
prayer wheels 13
precepts 9

refugees 21, 30

reincarnation 15, 30
retreats 21

sacred texts 22–23
Sangha 5, 17
Sarnath 8
shrine 13
Siddhartha 6–7
statues 4, 12, 27
stupa 26, 30
symbol 26, 30

temples 12, 30
Thailand 21
Thangka paintings 26, 30
Theravada Buddhism 10
Theravadan Sangha 22
Thich Nhat Hanh 21, 25
Three Baskets 22
Three Jewels 5
Three Poisons 5
Tibet 16, 20, 25
Tibetan offering rice 29

uplifting energy 23, 30

Wesak 17
Western Buddhism 11, 14
Wheel of Teaching 5

Zen Buddhism 11

Notes for parents and teachers

Religions guidelines

This book on Buddhism is an accessible introduction to the beliefs and practices of the Buddhist faith. It does not aim to be a comprehensive guide but gives plenty of opportunity for further activities and study. The content closely links with the non-statutory National Framework for Religious Education, and particularly the QCA schemes of work listed below. The topics selected also overlap with locally agreed RE syllabuses.

Unit 1A: What does it mean to belong?

Unit 1D: Beliefs and practice

Unit 2C: Celebrations

Unit 2D: Visiting a place of worship

Unit 3A: What do signs and symbols mean in religion?

Unit 4D: What religions are represented in our neighbourhood?

Unit 6A: Worship and community

Unit 6C: Why are sacred texts important?

Photographs

Use the photographs to encourage children to question, reflect and investigate further. Mount Kailas on page 25 is a holy mountain for both Buddhists and Hindus. It is in itself a wonderful teaching on interdependence. The five rivers that rise from Kailas flow all over Asia and irrigate the lands that feed 43% of the world's population. This amazing fact shows how important it is to look after and care for the environment.

Visiting a monastery

There may be a Buddhist monastery near where you live. Most monasteries do have visiting times, so give them a ring and ask what facilities are available. Remember to take off your shoes when entering the monastery and please show respect to the environment – many of them have beautiful, peaceful grounds.

More books to read

Prince Siddhartha
Jonathan Landaw and Janet Brooke,
Wisdom Publications 2003

The Jataka Tales
A series of story books for children,
Dharma Publishing 1989

Tenzin's Deer
Barbara Soros,
Barefoot Books 2003

Barefoot Book of Buddhist Tales
Sherab Chodzin Kohn,
Barefoot Books 1999

What Do We Know About Buddhism?
Anita Ganeri,
Peter Bendick Books 1997

Useful websites

www.clear-vision.org
Some interesting, relevant and appropriate resources for all age groups.

www.dalailama.com
A helpful site outlining the life, teachings and philosophy of an inspirational leader, His Holiness the Dalai Lama.

www.amaravati.org
More about the Theravadan Community.

www.wisdom-books.com
Books for parents, teachers and children.

www.buddha.net
A general site about Buddhism but including material and stories for children.

www.reonline.org.uk
A family of websites that looks at religious education resources for teachers.